WITHDRAWN

Fact Finders®

DISCOVER THE NIGHT SKY

EXPLORING
AURORAS

BY KAREN LATCHANA KENNEY

Consultant:
Ilia Iankov Roussev, PhD

CAPSTONE PRESS
a capstone imprint

Fact Finders Books are published by Capstone Press,
1710 Roe Crest Drive, North Mankato, Minnesota 56003
www.mycapstone.com

Library of Congress Cataloging-in-Publication Data
Library of Congress Cataloging-in-Publication data is available on the Library of Congress website.

978-1-5157-8734-1 (library binding)
978-1-5157-8738-9 (paperback)
978-1-5157-8750-1 (eBook PDF)

Editorial Credits
Adrian Vigliano, editor; Veronica Scott, designer;
Wanda Winch, media researcher; Gene Bentdahl, production specialist

Photo Credits
NASA, 21, IMAGE/UC Berkeley, 26, Johnson Space Center/Earth Science and Remote Sending Unit,
28–29 (background), Polar/University of Iowa, 7, Solar Dynamics Observatory, 14; Newscom: Mondadori
Portfolio, 16, Zuma Press/Peter Barritt, 17; Science Source, 11; Shutterstock: Aaron Rutten, 22–23,
Atiketta Sangasaeng, 10–11 (background), 27, Georgios Kollidas, 12, MidoSemsem, 8, Mihai Speteanu,
20, muratart, 14–15 (background), Nejron Photo, 24, Nicku, 10, Nicolas Primola, 19, Pavel Vakhrushev,
starfield background, Peter Hermes Furian, 13, Phung Chung Chyang, 4–5, 9, Tsuguliev, cover, 25,
Zulkefli Mohd Yusop, 18

Printed in the United States of America.
0101602R

TABLE OF CONTENTS

EXPLOSIONS OF LIGHT

On a cold night close to Earth's poles, gaze into the sky. Bright stars twinkle in the dark. Now watch — you are about to see the sky explode with color. Green light dances above the trees like flames. The light ripples in waves across the sky. Then other colors appear. First you see yellow, then red, and even blue. The lights swirl, and the sky shimmers.

What are those lights? This natural light show is an aurora. It can only be seen when it's dark in certain parts of the world. An aurora has different shapes. A curtain shape is thin and flat with folds. An aurora also moves in arcs, bands, and patches. An aurora can quickly change shape and color as it moves.

An aurora shoots upward through the sky. It is brightest at the bottom and gets fainter the higher up it goes.

Did You Know?

These lights were named after the goddess of dawn from Roman mythology. The goddess Aurora spread the rising sun's rosy rays of light.

Auroras happen in two areas on Earth, near the planet's poles. One is in the northern **hemisphere**. The lights here are the **aurora borealis**. Many people call them the northern lights. The best places to see the northern lights are in parts of Canada, Alaska, Iceland, and Norway.

Another area is in the southern hemisphere. These lights are the **aurora australis**, also called the southern lights. These lights are harder to see. They happen where few people live, over Antarctica and the southern Indian Ocean.

Auroras happen all year long. You just need a dark and clear sky to see them. Sometimes the lights are dim. Other times the lights are very bright. You could even read a book by their glow.

An auroral zone is the area where auroras happen. These zones are oval-shaped. They surround Earth's **magnetic poles**.

hemisphere—one half of the Earth; the equator divides the Earth into northern and southern hemispheres

aurora borealis—colorful bands of light in the sky of the northern hemisphere, also called the northern lights

aurora australis—colorful bands of light in the sky of the southern hemisphere, also called the southern lights

magnetic pole—one of two points on Earth's surface where its magnetic pull is the strongest; one is near the geographic North Pole and the other is near the South Pole

CHAPTER 2

DISCOVERING AURORAS

People have watched auroras for thousands of years, wondering what they could be. Were they a kind of lightning? Were they spirits in the sky? Were they reflections of the sun's rays? People wrote about the strange lights in the sky. Some people were frightened by auroras, believing they were signs of bad things to come. Different cultures made legends to explain what they were.

An early description of auroras was found on a clay tablet from Babylon. The ruins of this ancient city are in modern-day Iraq. The tablet describes a red glow in the night sky in 567 BC. Scientists believe it was an aurora.

Other records tell of these lights too. Ancient Greek thinker Aristotle wrote that the lights came from cracks in the sky. Later records from China and Japan describe red clouds with bands of white. These descriptions might have been referring to the rays auroras.

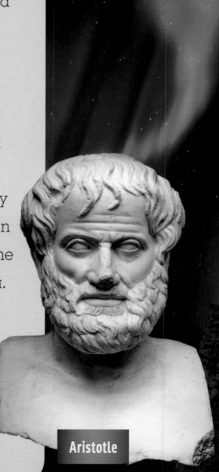

Aristotle

A Spirit Pathway

One **Inuit** legend explains auroras. It tells of a lighted pathway in the sky. Spirits hold torches in a line. The lights guide new spirits to a hole in the sky. It leads the spirits to the heavens. The spirits also feast and play soccer with a walrus skull. This makes the lights dance and move. The spirits try to talk with people on Earth by making whistles and cracking sounds. This describes the sounds people have reported hearing from auroras.

Inuit—people from the Arctic north of Canada, Alaska, and Greenland;

Scientists began studying auroras. They came up with different theories to try to explain them.

Some thought an aurora was a reflection of moonlight. Italian scientist Galileo Galilei believed water in the air reflected the light. French philosopher René Descartes thought ice crystals did so. Many people believed this theory, but it turned out to be wrong.

Galileo Galilei

Then scientists began to wonder if auroras might be connected to magnetism. It started with British scientist William Gilbert. In the year 1600, he published a book about magnetism. He experimented with magnets and believed Earth was a giant magnet too. It had magnetic poles, just like a magnet.

William Gilbert

Did You Know?

Gilbert used a magnet shaped like a **sphere**. He moved a compass around it. The needle always pointed to the north pole of the sphere. This is just how a compass acts on Earth.

sphere—a round, solid shape like a basketball or globe

British astronomer Edmond Halley was the first to connect auroras with magnetism. He had studied Earth's magnetism for the British navy. Then in 1716 he saw an amazing auroral display. It was the biggest one in a century.

Halley made scientific observations of the event. He saw that the aurora's curtain moved in a certain way. It moved in the direction that a compass needle pointed when hanging in the air. A compass needle always points toward Earth's North Pole. This discovery led Halley to connect the lights with Earth's magnetism.

Edmond Halley

He thought matter moved in a **magnetic field** around Earth toward the poles. Then it reacted somehow to make light. It explained why auroras only happen near Earth's poles.

magnetic field—the area around a magnet that can attract other metals or protect a planet from space particles

The Magnetic Earth

Scientists now know that Gilbert and Halley were right. Earth is a giant magnet. This is because of the planet's layers. At the core is a solid iron ball. Around it is a layer of moving hot liquid metal. Scientists believe that this moving liquid makes the planet magnetic.

From Earth's center a magnetic field exits through the South Pole. It moves around the planet and enters at the magnetic North Pole. From there the magnetic field goes back to the center of the Earth again. This forms a giant loop.

Compass

North magnetic pole

Geographic north pole

Magnetic axis

11,5°

Rotation axis

Crust
Stiffer mantle
Liquid outer core
Solid inner core

Geographic south pole

South magnetic pole

Magnetic field lines

Other scientists believed **electricity** in the air caused auroras. Lightning is a form of electricity. It lights up the sky too. Could it be the reason auroras happen?

Benjamin Franklin had experimented with lightning and electricity. He thought lightning might be similar to the northern lights. Franklin wrote a paper about his theory in 1778. He thought electricity moved in warm air. It traveled from tropical areas to the poles. The warm air had so much electricity that it released into the air as light. Other scientists believed in this electricity theory too.

Then on September 1, 1859, British astronomer Richard Carrington saw something strange. He was studying the sun and noticed bright white light. It erupted from giant spots on the sun called sunspots. Then it suddenly disappeared. Before dawn the next morning, brilliant auroras lit up skies around Earth. Scientists wondered if the sun was part of what caused auroras.

Another discovery would help explain an aurora's colors. British scientist Sir William Cooke experimented with gas to see how it glows. He found that moving **electrons** made gas glow. Different kinds of gases glowed in different colors. And a magnet attracted the glowing light. All of these discoveries added more clues to the mystery of an aurora.

electricity—flow or stream of charged particles, such as electrons

electron—a tiny particle with a negative electrical charge that moves around the nucleus of an atom

CHAPTER 3

Studying the Glow

Scientists had found pieces of the puzzle. The sun seemed to be involved. Earth's magnetism was important. Electricity was part of it too. But how were they all connected?

In the late 1800s, Norwegian physicist Kristian Birkeland made some important connections. He became a pioneer in aurora science. Birkeland watched auroras in northern Norway. He collected data on them. He studied Earth's magnetic field as well. Birkeland also experimented in his laboratory.

In 1896 he had a theory on what caused an aurora. He believed the sun was the energy source for auroras. He thought particles from the sun hit Earth's magnetic field. They moved toward Earth's magnetic poles and hit atoms in the atmosphere. They excited the **atoms** of the **atmosphere**, which caused the glow. Birkeland's theory was partly correct. It greatly advanced our understanding of auroras.

Kristian Birkeland

Polar Explorers

The poles were some of the last places on Earth explored by Americans and Europeans. In the late 1800s and early 1900s, expeditions set out to reach the North Pole. Their journeys were long and difficult. They were also filled with amazing views of the northern lights. These explorers later wrote about what they saw. American explorer Frederick Cook wrote a book about his voyage in 1911. He described the aurora as running, liquid fire that glittered in the sky.

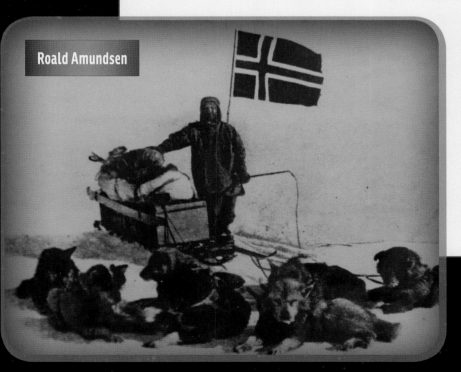

Roald Amundsen

Norwegian explorer Roald Amundsen explored the South Pole. He described the aurora as nature wearing its most beautiful dress.

atom—the smallest part of matter that determines all of its properties

atmosphere—the mix of gases that surround a planet

Another Norwegian scientist used math to explain auroras. Carl Störmer was interested in Birkeland's experiments. He thought about Birkeland's theories. Then Störmer figured out how electrons move in the magnetic field using math.

Störmer began taking pictures of auroras too. In 1909 he set up a system. He found sites in Norway. He connected them by telephone. Several people took photographs of an aurora at the same time. In the two pictures, the aurora appeared in different spots.

Störmer used the photographs to measure an aurora's height. He found the bottom of an aurora. He also found the top of an aurora's peaks. He concluded that the lights appear in the ionosphere. This is one of the upper layers of Earth's atmosphere.

ionosphere

Earth's atmosphere has several layers. People live in the troposphere. Auroras happen in the ionosphere.

troposphere

Scientists showed that electrons caused an aurora. They seemed to come from the sun, but how did they cause auroras? In the 1930s British scientist Sydney Chapman had a theory. He believed clouds of particles with an electrical charge flowed from the sun. We now call these clouds **plasma**, a kind of matter that exists in space. The plasma flows around Earth's upper atmosphere. Electrical particles in the plasma are part of what cause auroras.

Van Allen belts

Then in 1958, American space scientist James Van Allen found another important clue. He was part of a team that launched the first American **satellite** to orbit Earth. The satellite's instruments collected data about the atmosphere. Using the data, Van Allen found electrical particles trapped in the atmosphere. They collected in rings around Earth. Scientists call these rings the Van Allen belts.

plasma—a gas containing charged particles
satellite—a spacecraft that orbits a planet

CHAPTER 4

EXPLAINING AURORAS

The first satellites gave us clearer views of space. Since then our technology has gotten better. Scientists can study our planet, the sun, and space in more advanced ways. Satellites and rockets collect important information. Their images and data have confirmed theories about auroras. We now have proof about why they happen.

An aurora's energy starts at the sun. The sun is our star, and it is a burning ball of hydrogen gas. It is the biggest source of energy on Earth and in the solar system. The sun's atmosphere contains tiny particles. The particles move away from the sun as gases burn. They move toward Earth in what's called a solar wind. The solar wind is made of plasma.

Sometimes the sun releases a lot of energy. It erupts in a flare or coronal mass ejection (CME). This is what Carrington saw in 1859. A CME sends an explosion of energy rushing toward Earth at a few million miles per hour. A CME can trigger a very bright aurora on Earth.

The plasma from the solar wind hits Earth's magnetic field. This field stops many of the sun's particles from hitting Earth and protects the planet. The sun's particles also disturb the magnetic field, which contains charged particles. With so much energy, the field becomes out of balance. It creates an electrical current that releases particles into the atmosphere. The particles rush toward Earth's magnetic poles.

At the poles, the charged particles hit atoms. They transfer the energy to the atoms and excite them. The atoms then release the energy as light.

Different atoms produce different colors. Some oxygen atoms are lower in the atmosphere. This makes a green-yellow aurora. Oxygen atoms higher up make a red aurora. Sometimes an aurora is blue and red near its bottom. This color comes from hydrogen atoms. Hydrogen and helium atoms can also make a blue-purple aurora.

Aurora Chasers

People are drawn to the colorful beauty of auroras. They are magical sights to see. Some people chase them down every night. These aurora hunters watch weather data. They leave their warm homes on cold nights. They search the sky and hope there are no clouds. With a little luck, they find an aurora. They take stunning photographs and watch the show.

Scientists haven't discovered everything about auroras. They continue to research them. New technology has revealed more about these colorful lights.

Japanese scientist Shun-ichi Akasofu made a discovery using all-sky cameras. These cameras take black and white videos of the entire sky. The videos show an aurora from horizon to horizon. These tools can be used to see the sky from all parts of the world.

Akasofu used data from 100 all-sky cameras. He found that the northern and southern lights were mirror images. They look exactly the same, but are on opposite ends of the planet. Akasofu also found out more about the auroral zone. It is not a perfect oval over the magnetic pole, as previous scientists believed. It is lopsided.

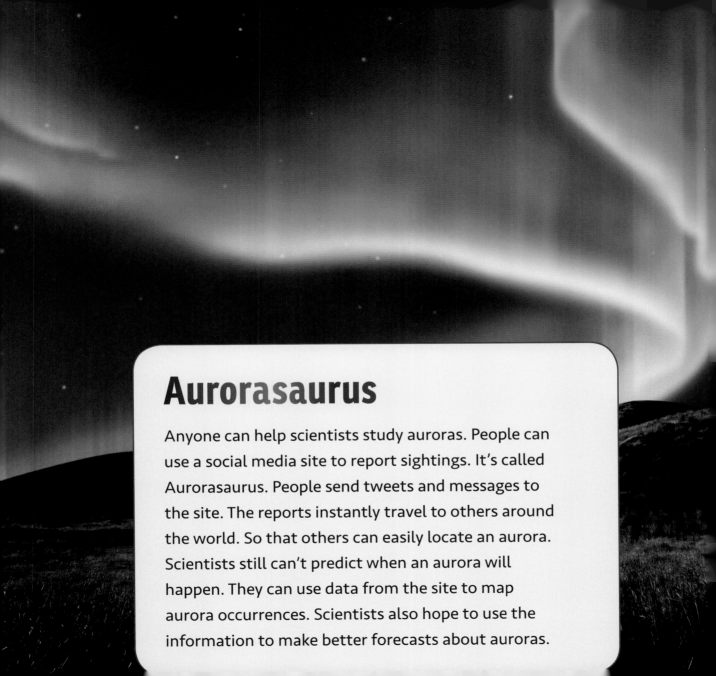

Aurorasaurus

Anyone can help scientists study auroras. People can use a social media site to report sightings. It's called Aurorasaurus. People send tweets and messages to the site. The reports instantly travel to others around the world. So that others can easily locate an aurora. Scientists still can't predict when an aurora will happen. They can use data from the site to map aurora occurrences. Scientists also hope to use the information to make better forecasts about auroras.

We've learned a lot about auroras from the ground. But the best views come from space. From up there scientists can see an aurora wrap around Earth. Its rays glow, reaching out into space.

Astronauts aboard the International Space Station have the best view. This station orbits around Earth. Astronauts live there and observe Earth from space. They take incredible videos and photographs of auroras. Satellites, such as the Suomi-NPP, also record auroras from space. These recordings help scientists see auroras better. But they do not help scientists learn more about the particles in auroras.

Rockets containing scientific instruments gather information about particles. Scientists shoot rockets through auroras. As the rockets move through them, they collect data about the particles there.

Some mysteries remain about auroras. Scientists still do not know how aurora's particles move as fast as they do. They also do not know why an aurora forms in thin sheets. Scientists continue to study these glowing lights in the night sky. Someday they may find out even more about auroras.

AURORA TIMELINE:
FROM SIGHTINGS TO DISCOVERIES

67 BC
m Babylon record an
clay tablet. It's the first
rd of an aurora.

AD 1600
William Gilbert states that
Earth is a magnet.

1716
lley sees an aurora. He
vith Earth's magnetism.

1778
Benjamin Franklin believes
electricity is part of an aurora.
Other scientists agree.

1896
Birkeland's theory
the sun with auroras.

1909
Carl Störmer sets up a system to
photograph auroras. He measures
the height of an aurora.

1930s
man has a theory about
. It carries electrical
rom the sun to Earth.

1958
James Van Allen discovers rings
of electrical particles encircling
the Earth

GLOSSARY

atmosphere (AT-muhss-fihr)—the mix of gases that surround a planet

atom (AT-uhm)—the smallest part of matter that determines all of its properties

aurora australis (uh-ROR-uh aw-STRAH-lihss)—colorful bands of light in the sky of the southern hemisphere, also called the southern lights

aurora borealis (uh-ROR-uh bor-ee-AL-iss)—colorful bands of light in the sky of the northern hemisphere, also called the northern lights

electricity (i-lek-TRISS-uh-tee)— flow or stream of charged particles, such as electrons

electron (i-LEK-tron)—a tiny particle with a negative electrical charge that moves around the nucleus of an atom

hemisphere (HEM-uhss-fihr)—one half of the Earth; the equator divides the Earth into northern and southern hemispheres

Inuit (IN-yoo-it)— people from the Arctic north of Canada, Alaska, and Greenland; they were once known as Eskimos.

magnetic field (MAG-nit-ik FEELD)—the area around a magnet that can attract other metals or protect a planet from space particles

magnetic pole (MAG-nit-ik POHL)—one of two points on Earth's surface where its magnetic pull is the strongest; one is near the geographic North Pole and the other is near the South Pole

plasma (PLAZ-muh)—a gas containing charged particles

satellite (SAT-uh-lite)—a spacecraft that orbits a planet

sphere (SFIHR)— a round, solid shape like a basketball or globe

READ MORE

Hunter, Nick. *Northern Lights.* The Night Sky: and Other Amazing Sights. Chicago: Heinemann Library, 2013.

Morey, Allan. *The Science Behind Wonders of the Sky: Aurora Borealis, Moonbows, and St. Elmo's Fire.* The Science Behind Natural Phenomena. North Mankato, Minn.: Capstone Press, 2017.

Rajczak, Kristen. *The Northern Lights.* Nature's Light Show. New York: Gareth Stevens Publishing, 2013.

INTERNET SITES

Use FactHound to find Internet sites related to this book.

Visit *www.facthound.com*

Just type in 9781515787341 and go.

Check out projects, games and lots more at
www.capstonekids.com

CRITICAL THINKING QUESTIONS

1. What happens to give an aurora its colors? What are those colors?

2. How does the timeline show you what scientists have learned about auroras? How is it different from what is explained in the main text?

3. The sidebar titled "The Magnetic Earth" describes why Earth is a magnet. How does this help you understand more about auroras?

INDEX